Baby Names

The Ultimate collection of the best baby names for boys and girls, their meanings, and origins!

Table Of Contents

Introduction 1

Chapter 1: Choosing Your Baby's Name 2

Chapter 2: Popular Baby Names and Their Meanings 8

Chapter 3: Rare and Unique Baby Names for Boys 32

Chapter 4: Sophisticated Names for Your Baby Girl 39

Chapter 5: Baby Names That Can Go Either Way (Boys/Girls) 42

Chapter 6: Name Combinations 49

Conclusion 55

Introduction

I want to thank you and congratulate you for downloading the book, "Baby Names".

This book contains helpful information about baby names, and how to choose the perfect one for your child!

Choosing the right name for your baby can be a difficult task. This should be an exciting task for any couple, but unfortunately for many it can be quite stressful and daunting.

This book provides some steps to help make the name choosing process a fun one for both you and your partner. It explains the considerations you need to take when choosing a name, and helps to simplify the decision process.

This book includes the origins and meanings of the baby names, to help you in making your decision! It also includes lists of the most popular names, unique names, sophisticated names, unisex names, and even shows you some good ways to combine names to make your child's name a unique one!

Thanks again for downloading this book, I hope you find it helpful in choosing the perfect name for your child!

Chapter 1:
Choosing Your Baby's Name

Choosing your baby's name is no easy task, especially for first-time parents. Since your baby's name will form part of his/her identity, you want it to be as beautiful as it is meaningful.

Below are some tips that will help you out in choosing your baby's name:

1. **Identify your baby's gender**

   Your chosen name must fit your baby's gender, and in order for you to pick a fitting name, you naturally would have to know your baby's gender first. Luckily for you, it is now easy to find out your baby's gender months before birth using ultrasound technology, five months into the pregnancy. This will give you ample time to decide on the name you're going to give your baby.

   Of course, knowing the gender of your baby ahead of time is optional. There are some parents who want the gender of their baby to be a mystery until birth. For parents who prefer not to know the gender of their baby right away, don't fret! You will find in the later chapter of this book some tips on how you could prepare a name for your baby even if you don't know their gender.

2. **Talk with your partner about it**

   Keep in mind that the name of your child is a big deal. It must be decided by you and your partner together, so don't forget to ask for his/her insights about it.

3. **Consider possible nicknames/abbreviations**

   Steer clear of names that would form embarrassing initials or nicknames, lest your child be mocked about it. Consider all possible nicknames for the name you've chosen.

4. **Name length**

   Another thing to consider is the length of your baby's name. Do you want it long or short? Some parents want their children to have as many middle names as possible, but note that your child might not want this in the long haul. Imagine your child agonizing to write 5 -6 names on every test paper or application form? If you're planning to give your child a long name, this is definitely something you may want to consider.

5. **Know the name's meaning**

   Good research will go a long way when it comes to giving your baby a name. After all, you wouldn't want to give your child a beautiful sounding name which you later on find out to mean "poo" or "thief", right? That could be very embarrassing for your child. If you already have a name in mind, make sure that you do some quick research as to its meaning (and make sure it has a good one).

6. **Consult available baby names' list**

   When you are a first time parent, chances are you have no idea what name you want your first child to have. You want it to be personal to you, but you still come up empty. That's where this book comes in handy!

7. Names as a legacy

There are parents who want their legacy to be embedded in their baby's name, and bearing the father's surname is not enough. They would want their children to be their "Jr." or "II, III, IV" and so on, especially if it's a boy. If it's a girl, many parents want to name their little girl after her mother, aunt or grandmother. That's perfectly fine.

8. Spelling

One way to make your child's name unique is by adding some spice to the name's spelling, that is, making it unusual. Some add harmless letters such as "e" and "h" (Mheleesa instead of Melissa) while others just double some letters ("Isabelle" "Fionna"). If you choose to vary the spelling of your child's name to make it sound more unique and sophisticated, just make sure that the spelling is not too complicated. Otherwise, you run the risk of your child's name being misspelled often, and you wouldn't want your child explaining and correcting them over and over again.

9. Pronunciation

You would want your baby's name to be easily pronounced. Pick a name that sounds sophisticated but can be pronounced without difficulty. Don't give names such as "Czechthunee" "Grauchjois". For one, people would get exasperated just by seeing them spelled, and most importantly, they sound weird in the worst way possible. Relieve your child the burden of having to carry this kind of name forever.

These are the characteristics of a name that's easily pronounced:

- It contains at least one vowel for every one-two syllables

- It does not exceed 5 syllables

- It does not contain more than one "x" or "z" except in doubles i.e. maxxie, lizzie

- It does not contain more than 3 succeeding consonant letters hence the previous example "Cze*chth*unee" "Grau*chj*ois". Exception: 3 succeeding consonant letters containing one to two letters which are silent ("Chloe") or functioning as a vowel (Ethyl, Zyril).

10. Baby names for twins, triplets and so on

Preparing a name for one child can be daunting enough, but preparing for two or more names for multiple children at one time can give you a serious headache.

Don't worry because we're here to help you out! If you are expecting a twin or a triplets, below are some name choosing tips for you:

- Choose a name and create two or three (depending on the number of your children) variations of the name you had in mind.

    For example, if you have Jenny in mind and you're expecting 3 girls, you can vary Jen into 1) Jenny 2) Jane 3) Jennifer 4) Jennilyn.

Name: Ed – 1) Edward 2) Eddie 3) Edu 4) Edwin

- Pick completely different but related names such as John Paul, Benedict and Francis (named after the last three Popes of the Roman Catholic Church), Castor and Pollux (the famous brothers in Greek Mythology).

- Pick completely different and unrelated names. After all, there is no hard and fast rule when it comes to naming your children. The fact that they are twins/triplets does not mean that they have to be named similarly. Go with what your heart tells you.

11. A name you and your child will love

A name you and your child will love is probably the most important consideration to make when choosing a name. Always choose a name that reminds you of beautiful things, the kind that is as beautiful as your child.

12. Have fun

The last but equally important step in choosing your baby's name is to have fun. Choosing your baby's name should not stress you out to the point of despair. Remember that more than choosing your baby's name, you should prepare to become good parents to your coming child. Choosing a good and fitting name for your child is just the first step to make towards that responsibility.

With all these tips at hand, choosing your baby's name should not be as daunting as you feared it would be. In fact, choosing your baby's name should be a fun moment!

Chapter 2:
Popular Baby Names and Their Meanings

There are parents who want their baby's name to be common and popular. Some people may raise their eyebrows over this, but having a popular name actually has its advantages. For one, a popular name can easily be remembered, and since it is widely accepted as a popular name, people are less likely to find it weird and complicated. A popular name is also a safe bet if you are not really that creative or experimental. After all, you can never go wrong with a popular name!

Below are the top 100 most popular names for girls and boys for the years 2013 – 2014.

Top 100 Names for Girls

1. Sophia – It is a name of Greek origin which means "wisdom". It was also used by European royalty during the Middle Ages.

2. Emma – It is a name derived from Germany which means "whole" or "universal". It became popular during the 19th century.

3. Olivia – A name that pertains to an olive tree

4. Isabella – It comes from the word "Isabel", which is a variation of Elizabeth. It means "devoted to God" in Hebrew.

5. Mia – The name was first popularized by an actress named Mia Farrow as a shorter version of "Maria". It has its roots in Latin which means "mine" or "wished-for child."

6. Ava - A form of "Eve". Its origin is uncertain, but it may be derived from the Latin word "avis," which means "bird", or it could be variation of the name Chava which means "life".

7. Lily – A name derived from the Lily flower, a flower symbolizing purity in Christianity. It may also pertain to a shorter variation of Lillian and Elizabeth.

8. Zoe - A name of Greek origin which means "life." When the bible was translated into the Greek language, Eve was transformed into Zoe.

9. Emily – This name was derived from the Latin word 'Aemilia', which means "eager." The name started to become popular in the 1970s.

10. Chloe – A variation of the Greek name "Khloe," which was used to represent Demeter, the goddess of agriculture, grains and fertility. The name means "blooming" or "a greenish shoot."

11. Layla – The origin of this name may either be Egyptian/Arabic. It can either mean "intoxication," or "dark beauty."

12. Madison – A name of English origin derived from "Madde", a medieval girls' name which is a variation of Madeleine.

13. Madelyn – It is a Greek term which means "high tower." It is also a French form of Magdalene, of the New Testament.

14. Abigail – It is a Hebrew term which means "a father's joy". The name also comes from a biblical character named Abigail, the beautiful third wife of King David.

15. Aubrey – The name came from the Germanic name "Alberic", a name pertaining to the king of the elves in German mythology. Aubrey is one of the most common feminine variations of a male name.

16. Charlotte – A feminine form of "Charles," Charlotte means "a petite woman". Since the name "Charles" became a royal favorite, Charlotte also became the name of many female royalties.

17. Amelia – It is believed to be a variation of the medieval names "Emilia" and "Amalia", which are names of Latin origin meaning "industrious" and "striving." It also has a Teutonic meaning which is "the defender."

18. Ella - A short variation of either Eleanor or Ellen, which means "light." It is also an English term meaning a "fair woman" and has a German translation of "all" or "other".

19. Kaylee – It is an American/ English term meaning "pure" or "keeper of the keys". It is also believed to be a variant of Kay or Kayla.

20. Avery – It is a name which is derived from "Alfred". It means "wise" when translated in French and "counselor" when translated in English. It can be used as a name for both boys and girls.

21. Aaliyah – It is a name of Arabic origin which means "exalted".

22. Hailey – It comes from a traditional last name "Hayley" derived from Hale or Hales (a remote valley). There is a place named Hailey in Oxfordshire.

23. Hannah – A Hebrew term for "grace of God" or "God's favor". Hannah is also a biblical character portraying the mother of Samuel.

24. Addison – A name derived from "Adam". It can also be a combination of the names "Adam" and "Alysson".

25. Riley – The name is derived from the Old English word *"ryge leah"* which means "wood clearing" or "valiant". It may also be a variation of the Irish name Reilly.

26. Harper – A name of occupational origin which means someone who plays the harp or a harp player.

27. Aria – The name has Italian, Hebrew and Teutonic origins. It means "air" or "lion of God". In music, an aria is a soloist in an opera. Its Teutonic origins suggest that the term is related to a "bird".

28. Arianna – A feminine name of Welsh origin which means "silver".

29. Mackenzie – It is a name popular for both boys and girls. It was originally a Scottish last name, though it is of Gaelic origin. The name means either "comely", "child of the wise leader" and "fire-born."

30. Lila – It is a name of Arabic origin which means "night".

31. Evelyn – Did you know that Evelyn used to be a boy's name? It is an English last name, which became a name

for girls over time. It can be considered as a blend of the two names "Eve" (which is probably why men stopped using this name) and Lynn.

32. Adalyn – A name of American origin, Adalyn means "noble".

33. Grace- It is a name of Latin origin which is often related to goodness and generosity. In Greek mythology, it signifies beauty, blossom, and joy.

34. Brooklyn – Thought to be a combination of the names "Brook" and "Lynn" in reference to New York City.

35. Ellie – A shorter variation of the names Eleanor or Ellen which means "shining light".

36. Anna – It is a name of Hebrew origin which means "gracious".

37. Kaitlyn – It is derived from a Greek word which means "pure".

38. Isabelle – It is a name of Spanish origin which means "God is my oath" or "Devoted to God".

39. Sophie – It is a name of Greek origin; a variation of Sophia which means "wisdom".

40. Scarlett - Traditionally an occupational name for someone who sells bright fabrics. Scarlett means "bright red."

41. Natalie – It is derived from the Russian name "Natalia" which means either "birthday" or "Christmas." It

started to become popular in France and England after the Ballet Russe came to Paris during the 1900s.

42. Leah – The name is of Hebrew origin which means "weary".

43. Sarah – It is a Hebrew word meaning "princess".

44. Nora – It is a name short for "Honora" a name of Anglo-Norman origin derived from the Latin word meaning "honor." It may also be a short variation for Eleanora, a Greek name which means "light." It is also a feminine form of Norman, a name popular in Scotland.

45. Mila – It is a Slavic term for "industrious" and likewise a Russian term for "dear one." It's a variation of the names Milena and Camila.

46. Elizabeth – It is another form of the Hebrew "Elisheba", the biblical wife of Aaron. The name means "God is bountiful". Elizabeth is also the mother of John the Baptist in the New Testament.

47. Lillian- A variation of Lily, A nickname derived from "Elizabeth".

48. Kylie – It is the feminine form of the male name "Kyle" which means "handsome" or "near the chapel".

49. Audrey – It is an Old English name which means "noble strength."

50. Lucy – It is a name of Latin origin which means "light" or "illuminate".

51. Maya – A Latin term which means "great" or "larger" and a Sanskrit meaning of "illusion." It also has its roots in Roman mythology as Maia, the daughter of Atlas. It was after this name that the month of May came about. It's a variation of the name May.

52. Annabelle - It is a combination of Anna (which means "name of a king") and the French word Belle (which means "beautiful").

53. Makayla – It is a variation of "Michael" who is the only archangel in the Bible. It is a name of Hebrew origin which means "who is like God?"

54. Gabriella – It means "Devoted to God" in Hebrew. It is also a feminine version of the name "Gabriel" which is very popular in Italy. Girls named Gabriella often use nicknames such as Ella or Gabby.

55. Elena – A variation of the name "Eleanor" which is a Greek name meaning "light"

56. Victoria – It is a Latin term which means "victory". Victoria is also the Roman Goddess of victory often associated with the Roman Goddess of war and destruction, Bellona.

57. Claire – Originated from a Latin term meaning "clear" or "bright." It started to become popular in the 19th century, as a variation of Clare.

58. Savannah – It is a Spanish term which is descriptive of a "treeless plain" or a grassy plain with only a few trees in tropical and subtropical areas.

59. Peyton – Originated from a place in Sussex, England. It also has a Latin equivalent which means "royal".

60. Maria – It is a Semitic-rooted name, the meaning of which is uncertain. Some say it is originally an Egyptian name derived from *mry* meaning "beloved". It is also possible that it is a name derived from the Latin *mare* ("sea") or *maris* ("male"). It can be a feminine variation of Mars, the Roman god of war. Maria can also be derived from the biblical character of Mother Mary, the earthly mother of Jesus Christ. Common as the name is, there is no conclusive evidence of its meaning or origin.

61. Alaina – A name of Irish origin which means "rock" or "handsome".

62. Kennedy - An English version of the Irish Gaelic name "Cinnéidigh" which means "helmeted chief." This is a name used by both boys and girls.

63. Stella – It is a Greek name which means "a star".

64. Liliana – It comes as a variation of Lily, a Latin derived word meaning "pure".

65. Allison – Of Teutonic origin, Allison is a word which means "noble" or "kind"

66. Samantha – A Hebrew derived name which means either "listener" or "name of God"

67. Keira – An Irish name which means "dark-haired"

68. Alyssa – A name of Greek origin meaning "Someone logical".

69. Reagan - An Irish surname which means "the little ruler" often used as a name for both boys and girls. It started to become popular during Ronald Reagan's presidency.

70. Molly – It is a name for a small freshwater fish that is popular as pets and has been bred in different colors. It is a name of Latin origin.

71. Alexandra – The feminine form of Alexander, a name of Greek origin which means "the helper and defender of mankind".

72. Violet – A name of either Italian or American origin which means "flower". Presently, violet refers to either the violet flower or the color designation violet.

73. Charlie – A name of English origin which means "free".

74. Julia – A name derived from the Latin term which either means "downy-haired" or "youthful".

75. Sadie – It is a name of English origin, often used as a nickname for Sarah (which means "princess"). Sadie is the biblical wife of Abraham and the mother of Isaac.

76. Ruby – It comes from Old French name *rubi, derived* from the Medieval Latin term *rubinus,* which means "red".

77. Eva – A variation of the Hebrew name Eve (which means life).

78. Alice – A name of English origin, Alice means either "noble" or "kind".

79. Eliana – It is a name which originated from France. It means "light" or "moon".

80. Taylor - It is a popular English surname which originated as an occupational surname for tailors. The word "tailor" is derived from the Old French word *"tailleur"* which means "a cutter".

81. Callie – It is a Greek name which means "most beautiful".

82. Penelope – Also means "weaver" in Greek. Penelope is also the name of Odysseus' wife who patiently awaits his return for 20 years in the famous literature *"The Odyssey"*.

83. Camilla – It is a name derived from a Latin term which means "attendant".

84. Bailey – A name of Teutonic origin meaning "able" or "a man who is capable".

85. Kaelyn – A variation of the name "Caelyn" which is an English name meaning either "meadow" or "waterfall pool".

86. Alexis – Of German origin which means "noble" or "light".

87. Kayla - The name is derived from the Irish term "caol" which means "slender".

88. Katherine - It is a Greek name which means "pure" or "virginal".

89. Sydney – A name of French origin which means "wide meadow". It is also the name of the capital of New South Wales, Australia.

90. Lauren – It is a name of Latin origin which is derived from the phrase "of Laurentum" which means from the place of the laurel leaves.

91. Jasmine – A name which originated from Persian term "Yasamen". It also pertains to the Jasmine flower, a climbing plant with fragrant flowers often used as a main ingredient in perfumes.

92. London – The name comes from the Latin word 'Londinium', a pre-Roman word which probably means "a place belonging to people called Londinios". In some languages, London is translated to mean "fierce".

93. Bella – It is a popular variation of the name "Belle", a Latin name which means "beautiful".

94. Adeline – It is a variation of the name "Adele", a French name which means "noble".

95. Caroline – It is a combination of the Latin derived named "Carol" (which means "a joyous song") and "Linda" (which means pretty).

96. Vivian – A name of Latin origin which means "full of life".

97. Juliana – A variation of the Latin name "Julia" which means either "downy-haired" or "youthful/ young".

98. Gianna – A Hebrew name which means "God's grace".

99. Skyler - It is a modern spelling or feminine variation of the male name "Schuyler", which was originally introduced in America during the 17th century by the Dutch settlers in New York.

100. Jordyn – It is a name of Hebrew origin which means "descend".

Top 100 Names for Boys

1. Jackson – A last name of Hebrew origin which means "the son of Jack."

2. Aiden – It is derived from the name of the Celtic sun god Aiden which in turn means "the fiery one". It was traditionally a boys' name but different feminine variations of this name are also popular among girls. The name has traces in Ireland.

3. Liam – It is a name derived from the Irish name "Uilliam" which means "a strong-willed warrior" or "protector". The Irish name "Uilliam" was in turn derived from the Frankish name "Willahelm" meaning "helmet of will." It's also a known nickname or variation of the name "William."

4. Lucas - A name of Latin origin and a variation of "Luke" or "Lucius" which means "light-giving" or "illumination." Luke is also a biblical character and the author of the third gospel of the New Testament.

5. Noah - A Hebrew name which means "rest" and "comfort." It is also a famous biblical character chosen by God to build the ark and bring with him two of every animal, destined to survive the great flood.

6. Mason – It was traditionally a French surname which was later on used in the Middle Ages by stoneworkers. The name Mason literally means "one who works with stone" or "a stoneworker".

7. Jayden - A modern combination of the names Jay and Hayden. The name Jayden has acquired its own meaning over time which is "Jehovah has heard."

8. Ethan – It is a Hebrew term for "strong" or "firm." Ethan is also a biblical character, who is described as a wise man.

9. Jacob – It is a name of Hebrew origin which means "supplanter". Jacob is also an important biblical character. He is the father of 12 sons who later on gave their names to the 12 tribes of Israel. Jacob has been in the popular names' list for more or less 30 years now.

10. Jack – The name started out as a nickname for the names John and James, which later on become a name in its own right. It has been commonly used to refer to any man from the working class. Due to its popularity in the Middle Ages, it was considered as a slang word which means "man".

11. Caden – A name of Arabic origin, Caden is a variation of the word "kadin" which means "friend" or "companion". In Welsh, "caden" is a word which means "the spirit of battle." Caden is also considered as a variation of McCadden, an Irish and Scottish surname.

12. Logan – It is a Scottish name which means "small hollow".

13. Benjamin – The name means "son of the South" or "son of my old age. The name is probably derived from the biblical character Benjamin who was the youngest of the 12 sons of Jacob. Many well-known personalities bear the name such as Benjamin Franklin.

14. Michael – It is a Hebrew name which means the rhetorical question "who is like God?". St. Michael is a biblical character who led the angels against Satan. He is now the patron saint of soldiers.

15. Caleb – Caleb comes from a Hebrew word which means "dog", a sacred animal used to symbolize endless devotion to God. Caleb is a biblical character who left Egypt together with Moses and is one among the only 2 followers who made it to the promised land.

16. Ryan – The name started out as a classic Irish last name which means either "descendant of the king," or "little king."

17. Alexander – It is a name of Greek origin which means "defender of men." It is believed to have been defined as such because of the countless kings and emperors, who adopted the name Alexander, and have ruled since the time of the ancient Greeks.

18. Elijah – It is a Hebrew term which means "Yahweh is God." Elijah is also a biblical character, an Israelite prophet in the Books of Kings. It became a popular Jewish name in the 1990s.

19. James – It is a name derived from the Hebrew name Jacob. It means either "supplanter," or "the one who follows". The name became more popular in the 17th

century when the King James VI inherited the English throne and became the first ruler of Britain.

20. William – Is a name which originated from Germany and became popular over England after several kings adopted the name. William means "a strong-willed warrior."

21. Oliver – The name is a variation of the French name "Olivier". It is derived from the Latin word "olivarius" which means "olive tree".

22. Connor – It originated from Ireland and was derived from the Gaelic name "Conchobhar". It also has a Scottish translation which means "wise."

23. Matthew – The name which has been popular since 1960s, originated from the Hebrew name "Matityahu" which means "a gift from God". Matthew is also a biblical character and was one of Jesus's apostles. Matthew is the author of the first Gospel in the New Testament.

24. Daniel – It is a name of Hebrew origin which means "God is my judge".

25. Luke – The name is a variation of Lucas which means "light giving" or "light giver". Luke is likewise the author of the third gospel in the New Testament. Later on, Luke became the patron saint of doctors and artists alike.

26. Brayden- It is a modern variation of the name Braden or Bradon. It started out as an English surname which means "someone from Bradden" or "someone who lives

near a broad valley". The name which originated from Ireland, can also means "broad," "brave," or "wise."

27. Jayce – The name originated from Greece. It means "healer" or "one who heals".

28. Henry – A name of German origin, Henry means "the ruler of the household". This is probably because 8 kings of England have adopted the name Henry.

29. Carter – The name started out as an occupational last name used by a cart driver, but later on became popular as a first name for boys.

30. Dylan – It is Welsh name derived from the Celtic word which means "sea." It became popular in the 1960s, when folk singer Bob Dylan rose to stardom.

31. Gabriel – A name of Hebrew origin, Gabriel means either "devoted to God" or "the hero of God" or "God is my strength". Gabriel is also a biblical character, the angel who told Virgin Mary that she would bear Jesus, the son of God.

32. Joshua – It is a Hebrew name which means "Lord is salvation".

33. Nicholas – It is a Greek name which means "victory of the people" or "the people won".

34. Isaac – It is a name of Hebrew origin which means "he will laugh". Isaac is likewise a biblical character, the son of Abraham and Sarah, who was nearly sacrificed by Abraham to appease God.

35. Owen - A popular Welsh name which means either "a young warrior" or "well born" or "noble." The name started to become popular in the year 2000.

36. Nathan – It is a Hebrew name which means "He gave".

37. Grayson – It started out as a popular English last name which means "son of a steward." It is derived from the Middle English word "greyve" which means "steward."

38. Eli – The name is a Hebrew word which means either "my God," "high," or "elevated." Eli is also a biblical character. He is a priest and judge who brought up Samuel the prophet. Eli started out as a boys' name but was later on used as a girls' name varied as "Ellie".

39. Landon – It started out as a last name for English people who lived in places called Landon. The name means either "long hill" or "ridge."

40. Andrew – It is a name derived from a Greek word which means either "strong," "manly," or "courageous." Andrew is also a biblical character in the New Testament, the first apostle to be called on by Jesus.

41. Max – It is a name derived from "Maximilian" which means "the greatest" and "Maxwell" which means "great spring".

42. Samuel – This is a name derived from a Hebrew word which stands for "heard God" or "asked of God." Samuel is likewise a biblical character, a prophet and judge who first established the Hebrew monarchy.

43. Gavin – It is a modern variation of the medieval name "Gawain" which means "white hawk." The medieval

name was used by Sir Gawain who was a knight of King Arthur's Round Table. It could also be derived from St. Gavinus, a popular Christian martyr.

44. Wyatt – It is a name which originated in France. It is an Old English name derived from "wido" which means "wood" or "wide". It started out as "Guyat" and "Wyat" during medieval times. It may also be a variation of the name "Wigheard", a combination of wig ("war") and heard ("brave ").

45. Christian – It is a name which means "a follower of Christ." Though it started out as a boys' name, it became popular as a girls' name in Scotland during the 17th and 18th centuries.

46. Hunter – The name was first used in Scotland and England during the Middle Ages as an occupational surname for hunters and bird catchers. It was only later on that Hunter became popular as a first name.

47. Cameron – It is a Scottish name which means "crooked nose".

48. Evan – It is a Welsh name of Hebrew origin derived from "Iefan" a variation of the name "John". It can also be a variation of names such as Juan, Ivan, Ian and Evangelos. It means "YHWH is gracious" in Hebrew.

49. Charlie – It is a name of English origin which means "free".

50. David – It is a Hebrew name which means "the beloved". David is also a biblical character, the man who was able to beat Goliath despite the latter's strength and size.

51. Sebastian – The name came from a Latin term which means "venerable" or "revered." The name gained popularity during the middle ages after St. Sebastian, a popular martyr.

52. Joseph – It is a Hebrew name which stands for "God shall add".

53. Dominic – It is a name derived from a Latin term which means "belonging to God" or "he belongs to God".

54. Anthony – It is a name of Latin origin which means "priceless".

55. Colton – It is an English name which was used to refer to a "town of colt-breeding". It became popular as a first name later on.

56. John – It is a name of Hebrew origin which means "God is gracious".

57. Tyler – It is a name of English origin which started out as an occupational last name "Tiler" which stands for "a maker of bricks or tiles".

58. Zachary – It is a Hebrew name which means "remembered by God".

59. Thomas – It is a name of Hebrew origin which means "a twin" or "the twins". St. Thomas a well-known saint, also contributed to the name's popularity.

60. Julian – It is a name of Latin origin which means either "bearded" or "father of the skies" in reference to a higher being.

61. Levi – It is a Hebrew term which means "joined in harmony." Levi is also a biblical character, the third son of Jacob. Levi was also the former name of Matthew before he joined Christ and became his apostle.

62. Adam – Adam in Hebrew means "red Earth".

63. Isaiah – It is a Hebrew word for "salvation of the lord". Isaiah is also a popular biblical character.

64. Alex – It is a shorter form of "Alexander" a name of Greek origin which means "helper and defender of mankind".

65. Aaron – It is a Hebrew name which means "enlightened" or "the enlightened one".

66. Parker - It was a last name of English origin given to someone who was a gamekeeper during the medieval times.

67. Cooper – It is of Latin origin which started out as an occupational name for people who make barrels. Cooper means "barrel makers" in Latin.

68. Miles – It is a Latin name which means "soldier".

69. Chase – It is a name which originated from France. It means "hunter" in referral to the hunter's job of "chasing" wild animals.

70. Muhammad – It is a name of Arabic origin which means "praised one".

71. Christopher – It is a Greek name which means "Christ-bearer".

72. Blake – It is a name of English origin which is used to refer to skin complexion either "dark" or "fair".

73. Austin – It is a Latin term which means "majestic dignity".

74. Jordan – It is a Hebrew name which means "descending". Jordan is also the name of a river in the Bible where Jesus was baptized.

75. Leo – It is Latin word which means "lion" and was the name of many Christian saints. The name became popular after it was adopted by several popes. It is also a short form of Leon or Leopold, which is a German word which means "brave people."

76. Jonathan – It is a name of Hebrew origin which means "God gives" or "God provides".

77. Adrian – The name is derived from a Latin term which means "dark one".

78. Colin – The name is derived from a Greek word used to refer to someone who is a victor.

79. Hudson – It is a name of English origin traditionally used as a last name which means "the son of Hudde", a popular first name during medieval times.

80. Ian – The name was first used in Scotland. It means "God is gracious".

81. Xavier – It is a name of Latin origin which means "savior".

82. Camden – It is a Scottish name which was used to refer to a "winding valley".

83. Tristan – It is a Welsh name which means either "the loud one" or "a loud man".

84. Carson – It is a Scandinavian name which was originally used to refer to someone who is a "Son of Carr".

85. Jason – It is a Greek name which refers to someone who is a "healer".

86. Nolan – It was traditionally a last name in Ireland. In Gaelic language however, Nolan refers to a descendant or kin of a chariot fighter or champion. In other languages, Nolan means either "famous" or "noble."

87. Riley – The name was derived from the Old English word "ryge leah" which means "wood clearing." It's also a variation of the name Reilly. The name Riley also means "valiant."

88. Lincoln – It is derived from a Latin term which means "lithe".

89. Brody – It is a name of Gaelic origin which means "ditch".

90. Bentley – It is an English name which was used to refer to someone who lives in or near the moor. It literally means "from the moor".

91. Nathaniel – It is a Hebrew name which means "gift of God".

92. Josiah – It is a name of Hebrew origin which means "fire of the Lord".

93. Declan – It is a popular Irish name which means either "man of prayer" or "full of goodness." It was named after St. Declan, the founder of a monastery in Ireland. St. Declan's Stone has been said to be the site of many miracles.

94. Jake – It is a variation or a shorter version of the Hebrew name Jacob which means "the supplanter".

95. Asher – It is a Hebrew name which means either "happy" or "blessed." Asher is also a biblical character, one of Jacob's sons. It is likewise a traditional name used to refer to someone who lived by an ash tree.

96. Jeremiah – It is a name of Hebrew origin which means "exalted of the lord".

97. Cole – It is a Greek term which means "victory of the people".

98. Mateo – It is a name of Spanish origin which means "gift of God". It is also a variation of the name "Matthew".

99. Micah – It is a biblical name which means "who is like God?" It is likewise a variation of the name Michael.

100. Elliot – It is a variation of the name Elijah which means "Lord is my God" It was traditionally used as a Hebrew last name.

Keep in mind that giving your baby a popular name doesn't mean the name is not well thought of. After all, a popular name got to be popular for a reason – it is a beautiful name, and many people find it as such!

Chapter 3:
Rare and Unique Baby Names for Boys

To some, choosing a name for a baby boy is much harder than it is to choose a name for a baby girl. Why so? Because a baby boy's name is often very direct - with very minimal embellishment. As such, you have to choose a name that is plain yet unique; a name fit for your precious baby boy.

The first thing that you have to know is how you can make your baby's name unique. Using the following techniques, you can definitely come up with a unique baby name that suits your style.

- Pick a common name, and twist its spelling

    - Instead of the common name Michael, you can come up with Mikael or Michail, a Hebrew term which means "who is like God?" implying that there is no other being comparable to God Almighty.

- Pick a rare name and combine it with a common name

    - If you feel like giving your child a unique name but you don't want it to sound too weird, pick a common name and combine it with a rare name. This way, you'll give a name that is both unique and familiar.

    - Examples: James Jin, (James which means "supplanter" and Jin a Chinese term which means "gold"

- Pick a place which holds special memories to you and vary its spelling. These are the so-called destination names. Below are some destination names that you can pick for your baby boy:

- London to Lyndon
- Paris to Parys
- Jamaica – Jamyka
- Alaska – Allasca
- Sydney – Sidni
- Orlando – Orlaindo
- Rio – Rieo
- Milan – Milano
- Berlin – Berlyn

- Surnames turned first names are slowly becoming a trend in choosing baby names. As you have learned in the previous chapter on popular baby names, most of the names therein were traditionally used as a last name. If you're running out of fresh ideas, you can pick a traditional last name and use it as your baby's first name.

To help you out, here is a list of 200 rare and unique baby names that you can choose from:

1. Agustin
2. Lev
3. Constantine
4. Rio
5. Arlo
6. Shepherd

7. Caspian
8. Demarcus
9. Alfred
10. Brysen
11. Braylin
12. Draven
13. Braylon
14. Ellison
15. Dangelo
16. Auden
17. Arian
18. Elian
19. Eliseo
20. West
21. Davon
22. Deon
23. Dimitri
24. Chester
25. Aurelio
26. Elvis
27. Enoch
28. Baxter
29. Benton
30. Bodhi
31. Anders
32. Willis
33. Flynn
34. Franco
35. Baker
36. Ethen
37. Freddy
38. Burger
39. Cajun
40. Casanova
41. Leopold
42. Teo
43. Ellington
44. Stetson
45. Thiago
46. Thirdy

47. Blaise

48. Brice

49. Stellan

50. Roscoe

51. Howard

52. Haiden

53. Bram

54. Gaige

55. Gibson

56. Cassidy

57. Penn

58. Houston

59. Hugh

60. Octavius

61. Slater

62. Graysen

63. True

64. Nile

65. Hendrix

66. Pax

67. Everest

68. Rufus

69. Ignacio

70. Orson

71. Casimir

72. Kingsley

73. Kamren

74. Laszlo

75. Jag

76. Nixon

77. Otto

78. Pierre

79. Kashmere

80. Ripley

81. Cub

82. Daxx

83. Danish

84. Keon

85. Kael

86. Kyan

87. Jaylon
88. Jabari
89. Hawk
90. Pascal
91. Kohen
92. Legend
93. Kazz
94. Kodiak
95. Lalo
96. Leviathan
97. Panda
98. Keyon
99. Fitzgerald
100. Legacy
101. Neon
102. Pate
103. Pawk
104. Joziah
105. Jaron
106. Shaw
107. Jakobe
108. Johann
109. Mercer
110. Jeramiah
111. Darryl
112. Donte
113. Ozias
114. Cobain
115. Hippo
116. Jedi
117. Zion
118. Coleman
119. Lorcan
120. Miggy
121. Osbaldo
122. Bowie
123. Miller
124. Mustafa
125. Larson
126. Cosmo

127.	Leighton		147.	Devan
128.	Legend		148.	Brecken
129.	Ajax		149.	Griffith
130.	Anibal		150.	Whit
131.	Alpha		151.	Coen
132.	Lathan		152.	Cristiano
133.	Hart		153.	Maguire
134.	Cadence		154.	Rafferty
135.	Rocket		155.	Maxton
136.	Tintin		156.	Mariano
137.	Clinton		157.	Maxx
138.	Crew		158.	Sacha
139.	Baobao		159.	Ball
140.	Braulio		160.	Bond
141.	Bright		161.	Cello
142.	Trace		162.	Kix
143.	Laird		163.	Damari
144.	Bridger		164.	Florian
145.	Corban		165.	Cheese
146.	Cayson		166.	Chow

167.	Apollo	184.	Holmes
168.	Caige	185.	Cortez
169.	Aero	186.	Poet
170.	Dragos	187.	Broderick
171.	Peregrine	188.	Aaren
172.	Maksim	189.	Ab
173.	Major	190.	Egypt
174.	Malaki	191.	Exodus
175.	Camilo	192.	Four
176.	Mango	193.	Popeye
177.	Mowgli	194.	Rogue
178.	Navaryous	195.	Hurricane
179.	Enno	196.	Ivory
180.	Finch	197.	Drifter
181.	Crusoe	198.	Elite
182.	Devid	199.	Espn
183.	Donathan	200.	Yash

These are just some of the rarest baby boy names that you can choose from. Keep in mind that you can always mix and match these names to create an even more unique name for your baby.

Chapter 4:
Sophisticated Names for Your Baby Girl

Choosing a baby girl's name may seem easy due to the abundance of available names out there. However, the abundance of available names can make it difficult for you to find a unique name for your little girl. Almost every name has been taken, with the exception of those very weird names that you would never ever dream of giving your baby girl.

Since giving a unique (and beautiful) name can be very difficult, you can try the alternative and aim for sophisticated names instead.

Below is a list of top 15 sophisticated baby girl names and their meanings:

1. Amanda - It is a Latin name which means "worthy of love". The name "Amanda" was first recorded on a birth certificate in England in the year 1212. The name was later on popularized by poets and playwrights.

2. Adeline – It is a name of German origin derived from the Old German word "athal" which means "pleasant" or "noble".

3. Alicia - The name is a Teutonic name which means "noble humor". The name Alicia can also be traced from the Latin word "Adalheidis" which means "nobility".

4. Bernice – It is a Greek name which means "bringer of victory".

5. Emma – Emma is a variation of the name Emily. It is derived from the German word "Ermen" which means "whole or universal".

6. Elaine – It is a name of Arthurian origin. In the legend of King Arthur, Elaine was the mother of Sir Lancelot's son Galahad. Elaine means "shining light" in French. It is likewise an Old French variation of Helen.

7. Fiona – It is a name of Gaelic origin which means "white or fair". It was first used by Scottish author William Sharp as a pseudonym – Fiona MacLeod.

8. Gayle – It is a variation of "Abigail", a name of Hebrew and Anglo-Saxon origins which means either "happy God" or "Father in rejoicing" or "a father's joy".

9. Grace is an English name derived from the English word 'grace' which in turn was derived from the Latin word 'gratia' which means "God's favor".

10. Irene – It is an American and Greek name which means "peace". Irene is also a known Christian martyr. Later on, the name Irene was borne by several Byzantine empresses.

11. Iris – It is a Greek word which means "rainbow". Iris is also the Greek goddess of the rainbow. It is also used to refer to the name of the iris flower or the part of the eye.

12. Julia - Julia is a Latin baby name which means "young one". It is a female variation of the name Julius.

13. Veronica – It is a Latin baby name which means either "true image" or "honest image". Veronica is also a biblical character - the maiden who handed a handkerchief to Christ on His way to Calvary. When Christ's likeness miraculously appeared on the handkerchief, the name Veronica was given the meaning "true image" or "true likeness".

14. Lynne – It is an English baby name which is derived from the Gaelic word "lann" which means "house" or "church". It is likewise a variation of the name "Lynette" an Arthurian Legend character who accompanied Sir Gareth on a knightly quest.

15. Frances - The name Frances is a Latin baby name which means either "one from France" or "the free one".

Keep in mind that these baby names can be combined together with other names for a more sophisticated package (more on this in the next chapter). These names do not only sound sophisticated, they also mean something that perfectly describes your little girl. Go ahead and take your pick!

Chapter 5:
Baby Names That Can Go Either Way (Boys/Girls)

Some parents want their baby's gender a mystery until the date of the birth. While you can do this, you should prepare for a name ahead of time. Not knowing the gender can make it difficult for you to choose a name beforehand, but it is possible if you know how to do it. While you can pick both a boy's name, and also a girl's name that you like, there is another option.

One way you can prepare a name for your baby without knowing its gender is by choosing a name that can go either way – be it a baby girl or a baby boy. These names are flexible enough to suit a girl or a boy so the gender should not bother you, whatever it may be.

Here are 100 unisex names as well as name variations to choose from:

1. Aston (M) /Ashton (F) which means "east town" or "ash tree settlement"

2. Arlie (M)/ Arlene (F) which means "from the hare's meadow"

3. Ariel (M) /Arielle (F) which means "lion of God"

4. Andie (M or F, it could go either as Andrew or Andrea) which means "man"

5. Alex (M) / Alexis (F) which means "defender of men" or "protector of mankind"

6. Marx (M or F) which means "of Mars, the god of war"

7. Joseph (M) / Josephine (F) which means "He will add"

8. Angelo (M) / Angela (F) which means "messenger" or "angel"

9. Addison (M or F) which means "son of Adam"

10. Adi (M or F) which means "jewel" or "ornament"

11. Ashley (M or F) which means "ash tree meadow"

12. Avery (M or F) which means "elf counsel"

13. Bernie (M or F) which means "brave as a bear"

14. Blaire (M or F) which means "field of battle"

15. Brett (M) / Beth (F) which means "an inhabitant of Brittany"

16. Ferg (M or F) which means "virile"

17. Cary (M) / Carey (F) which means "stream"

18. Carson (M or F) which means "a son who lives in a swamp"

19. Celeste (M) / Celestine (F) which means "heavenly"

20. Chris (M or F) which means "carrier of Christ"

21. Dominique (M or F) which means "of the Lord"

22. Franky/ Frankie (M or F) which means "Frenchman" or "free one"

23. Gayle (M or F) which means "happy God" or "rejoicing father"

24. Gwyn (M) / Gwen (F) which means "white snow"

25. Gabby (M or F) which means "woman of God"

26. Harry (M) / Harrie (F) which means "home" or "house ruler"

27. Haley (M or F) which means "a compound of hay"

28. Hayden (M) / Heidi (F) which means "heathen"

29. Holly (M or F) which means "beautiful and bright one"

30. Jayden (M or F) which means "Jehovah has heard"

31. Jordan (M or F) which means "descend" or "flow down"

32. Jun (M) / June (F) which means "protector of women and marriage"

33. Kendall (M or F) which means "royal valley"

34. Kim (M or F) which means "bold family"

35. Lee (M) / Leigh (F) which means "clearing" or "meadow"

36. Joey (M or F) which means "may Jehovah add"

37. Lin (M) / Lynne (F) which means "forest"

38. Jackie (M or F) which means "may God protect"

39. Loren (M) / Lauren (F) which means "of Laurel trees"

40. Louis (M) / Louise (F) which means "famous warrior"

41. Mackenzie (M or F) which means "child of a wise leader"

42. Merlin (M) / Marilyn (F) which means "sea fortress"

43. Miles (M or F) which means "boastful soldier"

44. Morgan (M) / Morgana (F) which means "bright sea"

45. Murphy (M or F) which means "sea warrior"

46. Neo (M or F) which means "new"

47. Nicky (M or F) which means "people's victory"

48. Noah (M or F) which means "long-lived"

49. Ollie (M or F) which means "olive tree"

50. Ori (M or F) which means "my light"

51. Peyton (M or F) which means "regal"

52. Riley (M) / Reilly (F) which means "valiant"

53. Kyle (M or F) which means "handsome"

54. Robbie (M or F) which means "famous"

55. Sam (M or F) which means "child of the sun"

56. Tracy (M) / Tracey (F) which means "bold"

57. Shannon (M or F) which means "wise river"

58. Sidney (M or F) which means "from the place Saint-Denis"

59. Steph (M) / Stephanie (F) which means "crowned victory"

60. Steve (M) / Stevey (F) which means "crown" or "victorious"

61. Taylor (M or F) which means "cutter"

62. Terry (M or F) which means "ruler of the people"

63. Tom (M) / Tim (F) which means "twin"

64. Val (M or F) which means "strong"

65. Victor (M) / Victoria (F) which means "winner"

66. Will (M) / Wilma (F) which means "desire"

67. Zayn (M or F) which means "beautiful" or "pretty"

68. Martine (M or F) which means "war-like"

69. Ray (M or F) which means "mighty protection"

70. Ronnie (M or F) which means "mighty counselor"

71. Marlin (M) / Marlene or Marlyn (F) which means "dweller at the famous land"

72. Alexis (M or F) which means "to help and defend"

73. Blair (M or F) which means "dweller of the plain"

74. Casey (M or F) which means "brave"

75. Darryl (M or F) which means "darling"

76. Dylan (M or F) which means "son of the sea"

77. Dakota (M or F) which means "ally" or "friend"

78. Johnson (M or F) which means

79. Evan (M or F) which means "youth warrior"

80. Drew (M or F) which means "manly"

81. Glean (M) / Glenda (F) which means "secluded valley"

82. Hayley (M or F) which means "from the hay meadow"

83. Jesse (M or F) which means "wealthy"

84. Jan (M or F) which means "God is gracious"

85. Jamie (M or F) which means "supplanter"

86. Jade (M or F) which means "stone of the side"

87. Kendall (M) / Kendra (F) which means "valley of the river Kent"

88. Kelly (M or F) which means "warrior"

89. Nevada (M or F) which means "snowy"

90. Paris (M or F) which means "lover"

91. Perry (M) / Perrie (F) which means dweller by the pear tree"

92. Quinn (M or F) which means "fifth"

93. Reese (M or F) which means "ardor"

94. Robin (M or F) which means "bright fame"

95. Rene (M) / Renee (F) which means "reborn"

96. Sage (M or F) which means "wise"

97. Sean (M or F) which means "God is gracious"

98. Tracy (M) / Tracey (F) which means "harvester"

99. Wyn (M) / Wynne (F) which means "fair" or "white"

100. Zane (M or F) which means "gift of God"

Preparing for alternative names for your baby will make the task of choosing a name easier for you, especially if you didn't want to know the gender beforehand.

Chapter 6:
Name Combinations

Who said you should only give one name for your precious little one? You may have thought of a popular name, but you can make it unique by simply practicing the art of name combinations. Combining names will make it less likely that your child will contend with too many similar names. To many, name combinations sound more stylish.

Here are some tips and ideas for combining two or more names:

- **Combining your parents' names**

    Some people are sentimental when it comes to names. Others would have their baby named after their parents. If you like this idea, you can try combining your parents' names. For example, if your father's name is Jerry and your mother's name is Silvia, you can name your baby Jevia or Jessy.

- **Combining short and long names**

    If you're planning to give at least two first names to your baby, it is very important to consider the length of the names. You might want to combine one short and one long name so that it doesn't sound too long or too short. Combining two long names, i.e. Katherine Dorothy, would sound a little too wordy. On the other hand combining two short names, i.e. Zoe Liz would sound like it's composed of only one name instead of two. To make it sound more pleasing, combine one long and short name together, i.e. Zoe Katherine, Dorothy Liz, etc.

- **Combining two different names by taking their initial/end syllable**

  A more creative way to combine names is by taking two different names through their initial / end syllables to come up with one name. Below are some name combinations of this type:

  1. Adelinde (F) – A combination of Adel and Linda or Adel/Lynden
  2. Maricor (F) - A combination of Mary and Cory
  3. Jaysan (M) - A combination of Jay and Sandy
  4. Martine (F) - A combination of Marie and Christine
  5. Amberly (F) - A combination of Amber and Kimberly
  6. Maybeline (F) - A combination of Mabel and Lynne
  7. Kristofer (M) - A combination of Kristoff and Toper
  8. Amelia (F) - A combination of Amy and Emily
  9. Analee (F) - A combination of Ana and Lily
  10. Anjeanette (F) - A combination of Angie and Jeanette
  11. Ashley (M or F) - A combination of Ash and Lee
  12. Beatrice (F) - A combination of Bea and Bernice
  13. Billie (M) - A combination of Bill and Willie
  14. Brandy (M) - A combination of Brandon and Andy

15. Cady (M or F) - A combination of Caty and Cody

16. Carlene (F) - A combination of Carla and Arlene / Lyn

17. Charlie (M or F) - A combination of Charles / Charlotte and Billy / Ellie

18. Cheryl (F) - A combination of Cherry and Beryl

19. Clarybel (F) - A combination of Claire and Belle

20. Devaun (M) - A combination of Dave and Von

21. Freddy (M) - A combination of Fred and Eddie

22. Jaxine (F) - A combination of Jackie and Maxene

23. Kaylee (F) - A combination of Kay and Lee

24. Kendra (F) - A combination of Ken and Sandra

25. Lilybeth (F) - A combination of Lily and Elizabeth

26. Marlin (M or F) - A combination of Mario / Mary and Franklin / Lynn

27. Liam (M) - A combination of Lyndon and William

28. Roxanne (F) - A combination of Roxy and Anne

29. Wendell (M) - A combination of Owen and Del

30. Wynson (M) - A combination of Alwyn and Jackson

31. Gerald (M) - A combination of Gerry and Ronald

32. Jericho (M) - A combination of Jerry and Echo

33. Christiano (M) - A combination of Christian and Lino

34. Alfred (M) - A combination of Al and Freddie

35. Jovin (M) - A combination of Jose and Alvin

36. Henrix (M) - A combination of Henry and Felix

37. Lydia (F) - A combination of Lynn and Olivia

38. Maisee (F) - A combination of May and Daisy

39. Abigail (F) - A combination of Abby and Gayle

40. Justine (M or F) - A combination of June and Christine

41. Elizabeth (F) – A combination of Elise and Beth

42. Carminda (F) - A combination of Carmine and Linda

43. Nathaniel (M) - A combination of Nathan and Daniel

44. Genevive (F) - A combination of Gene and Olive

45. Jommell (M) - A combination of Jom and Romel

46. Joanna (F) - A combination of Joan and Anna

47. Leanne (F) - A combination of Lea and Anne

48. Scarlette (F) - A combination of Scar and Yvette

49. Gavin (M) - A combination of Garette and Alvin

50. Aldwin (M) - A combination of Al and Edwin

51. Camilla (F) - A combination of Camille and Ella

52. Marice (F) - A combination of Marie and Alice

53. Annabeth (F) - A combination of Anna and Beth

54. Angelica (F) - A combination of Angel and Lyca

55. Benedict (M) - A combination of Ben and Dickson

56. Roshelle (F) - A combination of Rose and Michelle

57. Theodore (M) - A combination of Theo and Dory

58. Lawrence (M) - A combination of Loren and Rence

59. Jeremy (M) - A combination of Jem and Romy

60. Jamie (F) - A combination of Jam and Amy

61. Katherine (F) - A combination of Kathy and Irene

62. Jaysen (F) - A combination of Jasmine and Sonia

63. Michelle (F) - A combination of Mitch and Rochelle

64. Kathryn (F) - A combination of Katrina and Dorine

65. Shaina (F) - A combination of Shane and Ina

66. Isabelle (F) - A combination of Isa and Belle

67. Ivaniel (M) - A combination of Ivan and Daniel

Combining names to come up with a new name is one of the best ways to make sure that your child will have a unique and meaningful name. Go on and try as many name combinations as you like to come up with the perfect name for your precious baby!

Conclusion

Thank you again for downloading this book!

I hope this book was able to help you in choosing a baby name!

Finally, if you enjoyed this book, please take the time to share your thoughts and post a review on Amazon. It'd be greatly appreciated!

Thank you and good luck!

www.ingramcontent.com/pod-product-compliance
Lightning Source LLC
LaVergne TN
LVHW021738060526
838200LV00052B/3343